Lake Placid and North Elba

A History 1800 - 2000

BY MARY MacKENZIE

Published by
The Bookstore Plus
Lake Placid, NY

Printed by Patterson Printing
Benton Harbor, Michigan

ISBN: 0-9719928-7-8

Library of Congress Control Number: 2002104627

Placid Lake, Mirror Lake, Village of Lake Placid, plains of North Elba and high peaks of the Adirondacks, c. 1930.
At upper left is Mt. Marcy, New York's highest mountain.

Preface

The Town of North Elba, with an area of 157.32 square miles and 100,685 acres, is situated on the extreme west line of Essex County, New York, and is contained in Townships 11 and 12 of the Old Military Tract. This area lies within New York State's great Adirondack Park.

It is predominately a wide and lofty plateau, encircled by the highest summits of New York's highest mountains, the Adirondacks. The Adirondack massif is classed as one of the most ancient mountain systems of the planet Earth and is of interest to both scientist and rockhound.

North Elba was traditionally the site of a Mohawk Indian summer village before the advent of the white man, and numerous artifacts unearthed over the years confirm the legend. After the Revolutionary War title to the entire Adirondack area passed to the sovereign State. North Elba was first included in Albany, Charlotte, Washington and Clinton counties, in succession, and finally Essex. Following the formation of Essex County in 1799, North Elba was part of the town of Elizabethtown until 1808 and then of Keene until 1850.

The "forever wild" State Forest Preserve comprises 75.7 percent of North Elba's area and only 24.3 percent is in private ownership. The private lands include two villages, Lake Placid and part of Saranac Lake, the hamlet of Ray Brook, the outlying settlements known as Averyville and Cascadeville, and occupied suburbs on the fringes of the villages, outside corporation bounds.

The Village of Lake Placid, noted summer and winter resort, 1.967 feet above sea level at its highest elevation, lies in the northern center of North Elba on the shores of lakes Placid and Mirror and overlooking the dense State woodlands and the scenic high peaks. Both geographically and historically, it has close ties with its township.

The Village of Saranac Lake, only nine miles to the west, has a somewhat different terrain, and bonds historically with the town of Harrietstown in Franklin County.

The recorded history of this beautiful region begins in 1800.

No. 22

James M. Intyre is entitled to Two hundred & forty Shares in the Stock of the **Elba Iron and Steel Manufacturing Company**, transferable at the Office of the Treasurer of said Company, by the said Stockholder, or by his Attorney; subject, nevertheless, to the further payment of forty-four ———— Dollars on each share, in such sums and at such times as the same shall be required.

Witness whereof, the Seal of said Company is hereunto affixed. Albany, the 6th day of August 1812.

By order of the Board of Trustees,

Arch. M. Intyre, Treas.r

PRINTED AT THE OFFICE OF *THE ALBANY REGISTER.*

Stock Certificate of Elba Iron & Steel Co. 1812.

ADIRONDACK MUSEUM

The Early Years

It was 1800. The Revolution was over and the great Yankee Exodus was on. Hordes of New England farmers were swarming over Lake Champlain to the howling wilderness of northern New York.

By the late 1790s a primitive wagon track, known as the Northwest Bay-Hopkinton Road, was in place from Westport on Lake Champlain to Hopkinton in St. Lawrence County. It was the first road to penetrate and cross the Adirondack wilderness.

Traveling this road in the spring of 1800, Elijah and Rebecca Bennet of Orwell, Vermont arrived on the lofty plateau of Lake Placid and North Elba. In tow were five children, their little daughter Laurillia and four offspring of Elijah's first marriage. Six more children would be born before 1810. Elijah, born in Connecticut in 1754, was a Revolutionary War veteran and had been severely wounded at the famous Battle of Bunker Hill.

Here at North Elba in prehistoric times, the Mohawk Indians had maintained a summer encampment for untold years, but the Bennets were Lake Placid's and North Elba's first permanent settlers.

The land, owned by the State of New York, was theirs for the choosing, and the Bennets chose well.

Archibald McIntyre, founder of the Elba ironworks.

ADIRONDACK MUSEUM

They settled on a good plot of land near present Power Pond on the Chubb River and probably within present village limits. They were soon joined by other New England farmers of that great Yankee Exodus.

By 1810, 200 pioneers and their numerous log cabins and barns inhabited a widely scattered community known as "The Plains of Abraham" on the fringes of the present Lake Placid Village and then within the town of Keene.

Fanny Dart was teaching in a log schoolhouse and Rev. Cyrus Comstock, an Essex County Congregational circuit rider, was providing sustenance for the soul.

The first marriage was that of Elijah McArthur and Electa Brooks. The first death was that of Arunah Taylor, who perished "by cold in the woods". In 1810, the next to go at the age of four, was little Eunice Needham. Hers is the earliest grave in North Elba Cemetery.

The earliest settlers were at first obliged to "squat" on their lands. North Elba was contained in Townships 11 and 12 of the State's Old Military Tract, which had never been surveyed into individual, saleable lots. In 1804 and 1805 the State sent surveyor Stephen Thorn up to accomplish the job so that patents could be issued. "Lake Placid" made its first appearance on Thorn's 1804 map. Whether the name was chosen by the settlers or by Thorn himself is unknown.

In 1811, the Chubb River was dammed and a substantial ironworks, mainly the creation of State Comptroller Archibald McIntyre, was erected on the present Power Pond. The two forges under one roof, grist mill, sawmill, barn barracks and numerous other buildings, were known as the Elba Ironworks. The name Elba was derived from the Mediterranean island of Elba, a rich source of minerals from ancient times and soon the site of Napoleon's exile. Ore for the works was mined down at Cascade Lakes. Many workmen poured into town and the population soon rose to close to 300.

Cascade Lakes pass in the town of Keene, site of the Elba iron mine.

The little outpost prospered. Though wolf, moose and panther had to be fended off and long, cold winters endured, the soil was extremely fertile and the ironworks provided a ready market for farm produce. The farmers also began to manufacture charcoal for the works.

The iron ore at Cascade Lakes mine soon proved inferior in quality, and the ironworks was forced to purchase its raw material at the great Arnold Hill mine in Clintonville, Clinton County.

In 1814, war came to the northland. Twelve men at the Plains joined the militia and fought in the renowned Battle of Plattsburgh in the War of 1812. One, James Wilson, was killed in action.

Growth continued until 1817, when two calamities led to a general exodus from the beautiful Plains of Abraham. The ironworks shut down for good, leaving scores without work, and the glacial weather of 1816, that infamous "Year Without A Summer" in the northern hemisphere, brought ruined crops and near starvation.

Now almost the entire colony moved out. The Plains of Abraham became virtually a ghost town, and a ghost town it would remain for the next quarter of a century. Only one of the original pioneers remained permanently—the Iddo Osgood family.

Daniel Ray left behind the name Ray Brook and Joseph Chubb the name of Chubb River. The Bennets stayed on until Elijah's death on December 17, 1830 at the age of 76. They left behind the name Bennet's Pond. That name would endure until the early 1870s, when the pond was rechristened Mirror Lake.

A few new families occasionally drifted in and out of the Plains, but no more than ten families were in residence at any one time. Four of the newcomers did remain permanently.

The Jacob Moodys arrived in 1819 at the town's far western limits, becoming the first settlers of the village of Saranac Lake. Also in 1819, the Simeon Averys settled in the Averyville section.

"Cort" Moody, one of North Elba's famous guides.
ADIRONDACK COLLECTION, SARANAC LAKE FREE LIBRARY

The Roswell Thompson family, which would achieve fame because of a close alliance with John Brown, arrived in 1824 and settled at the base of Cobble Hill. The old Thompson farmhouse stood at the junction of today's Northwood and Wilmington roads.

In 1837, the Moses Sampson family came to Ray Brook. Daniel Ames of neighboring Wilmington married daughter Jane in 1839 and the Ameses took over the farm. The old Ames farmhouse, built in the late 1840s, still stands opposite the Saranac Lake golf course. Ames started the thriving lumbering business that would be the mainstay of Ray Brook for the next half century.

These four families, along with Iddo Osgood, were the grassroots of what would soon be known as North Elba.

Isabelle Thompson Brown and son Freddy in 1860.
Isabelle, daughter of early settler Roswell Thompson, married
John Brown's son, Watson.

A Second Start

In the 1840s a second tide of immigration, this time from the neighboring towns of Essex County, was initiated at the Plains, a trickle at first and then a steady stream. It began in January of 1840 with the arrival of Remembrance Nash from Willsboro and, later that year, of Robert Scott from Keene and

Thomas and Polly Brewster came to North Elba in 1841.

Horatio Hinckley from Lewis. In 1841, Thomas Brewster and Alonzo Washburn came from Jay. The later 1840s saw the arrival of many more, including William Peacock, Nelson Blinn, Martin Lyon, Reuben Davis, John and Moses Huntington, James Merrill, Jacob Wood and Roswell Parkhurst. All of these newcomers and their descendants would contribute much to local history.

Horatio Hinckley farmhouse, Bear Cub Road, now part of Heaven Hill farmhouse.

The new influx was largely due to Gerrit Smith's sudden offer for sale of his inherited and purchased lands. Smith was a wealthy landowner and abolitionist of Peterboro, New York. Back in 1815 and 1817, his father, Peter Smith, a former partner of John Jacob Astor in the fur trade, had purchased a scattering of North Elba lots from the State. These Gerritt inherited in 1837. In the early 1840s he

Gerrit Smith

purchased from the State most of the remainder of North Elba except for the high peaks area, becoming practically the sole landlord of the town. Smith also founded a black colony here. As a humanitarian gesture, he gave away over 400 plots of 40 acres each to free black residents of New York State in 1846. There were never any escaped slaves or underground railroad activities in North Elba. Only about 15 black families actually settled here, and then not all at the same time. Life in the wilderness and the hard lot of a farmer had little appeal for these people. The colony dwindled away year by

year. By 1871, all were gone except the Lyman Epps family, which remained permanently.

Lyman Epps, Jr. about 1941, last local survivor of North Elba's black colony.

Short-lived as it was, the colony now receives national attention because of the widespread interest in black history.

This project did serve to draw the attention of the noted abolitionist John Brown. Wishing to instruct the blacks in good farming practices, he moved to the Plains with his family in June of 1849. The Browns moved to Ohio in 1851, returning here in 1855. John soon became embroiled in abolitionist activities in Kansas and elsewhere. He was seldom at North Elba for the next four years except for brief visits with his family.

John Brown in 1857. He did not grow the famous beard until the last of his life.

Mary (Mrs. John) Brown and daughters Annie, left and Sarah, right, 1851.

The Harper's Ferry incident, John Brown's hanging and his burial here focused national attention on North Elba and gave it considerable notoriety. The Brown farmhouse and grave site, two miles from Lake Placid, is now one of the world's great shrines. A State historic site, it was recently designated a National Historic Landmark.

The Roswell Thompson family established close ties with John Brown. Two of Brown's children were married to children of Roswell (Ruth to Henry Thompson and Watson to Isabelle Thompson). Also, Roswell's sons Dauphin and William went to Harper's Ferry with Brown and were killed in the raid.

By 1849, the settlement numbered about 40 families and 210 people. It was still known as The Plains of Abraham and was still in the town of Keene. Mail was delivered by post horse and rider from Keene Center. In October of 1849 the United States Government determined to give the settlement its own post office. A name had to be chosen. It seems obvious the difficult name The Plains of Abraham would have been quickly rejected. While there is nothing of record as to why Elba was chosen, it seems clear it was derived from the old Elba ironworks. When it was found that an Elba already existed down in Genesee County, the North was added.

Iddo Osgood had opened the first inn for travelers before 1833, just west of the present Uihlein Mercy Center, and it became the site of the new post office. Iddo's son Dillon Osgood was appointed the first postmaster on November 19, 1849.

William Thompson   *Dauphin Thompson*
North Elba men killed during John Brown's raid at Harper's Ferry.

Less than a month later, on December 13, 1849, the Essex County Board of Supervisors passed a resolution to set off the area from Keene as a separate township under the name of the post office, North Elba. The resolution took effect January 1, 1850. The first town of North Elba meeting, for the election of officers, was held on March 5, 1850 and John Thompson, son of Roswell, was elected the first supervisor.

Thus, after half a century, did the name The Plains of Abraham cease to be.

Within two years North Elba became even larger in area. By action of the Board of Supervisors, a good-sized chunk of land was taken off from the south end of the town of St. Armand and added to the north border of North Elba. It contained more of Placid Lake, and also McKenzie Pond, the Moody land and all the rest of Saranac Lake now within North Elba.

But something else was astir, quite out of the ordinary—something to talk and wonder about but of little significance then for it bore no relation to the exigencies of farm life.

As early as the mid-1840s outlanders began to appear on the farm roads. Artists, writers, mountain climbers, sportsmen and professional people were trickling in for a look at the unspoiled wonders of the wild. The outside world had discovered the Adirondacks.

It was the beginning of what would, in the end, totally consume, engage and define Lake Placid and North Elba for all time.

The first recorded visit to North Elba was that of Richard Henry Dana, Jr., famous author of *Two Years Before The Mast*. He stayed at Osgood's inn in June of 1849. There were few places of accommodation in those early years. Beginning about 1850, Robert Scott's farmhouse on the road to Keene doubled as a wayside inn. At the Saranac Lake end of the town, Colonel Milote Baker erected a small hotel in 1852. But catering to summer tourists would soon become a way of life for many an Elba farmer.

Also, over the years, guiding would become an important and lucrative sideline and North Elba's Moody boys and Bill Nye achieved considerable fame as Adirondack guides.

Up to this time there had been no settlement around lakes Mirror and Placid aside from the early and short tenure of Elijah Bennet's son Oliver. In 1850, the main roots of the village of Lake Placid were laid down with the purchase of large tracts on the west shores of Mirror Lake by Joseph Vernon Nash, a son of Remembrance Nash. His 320 acres of farmland, bought for a mere $480, would fetch a king's ransom today. His land encompassed what is today the main business section and a large residential block—all of Main Street from the Hilton complex down to the Olympic Oval, all of Grand View Hill and some of Signal Hill.

In 1851, Benjamin Brewster, son of Thomas Brewster, joined Nash on Mirror Lake. He acquired a large tract of land bordering Nash on the north, and including most of Signal Hill over to Placid Lake.

Nash married Benjamin Brewster's sister Harriet, and the couple first lived in a log cabin on the lake shore. In 1852, they built a farmhouse on the site of the present Hilton Motor Lodge. In 1855, with Yankee ingenuity, Nash enlarged the house and turned innkeeper for the spiraling tourist trade. Overnight, the Nash inn, always known as "the Red House", became the place to stay. For the next quarter of a century hordes of the talented, well-known and well-heeled would pass through its doors.

Joseph V. Nash   *Benjamin Brewster*
First settlers of Lake Placid Village.

Earliest known photo (1860s) of the Nash farmhouse, first house in lake Placid Village.

Lake Placid Village in 1873. The Joseph V. Nash farmhouse and barns occupy the site of the present Hilton resort.

Out on the old Plains of Abraham, in 1864, Martin Lyon opened a little stagecoach inn known as the North Elba House. Still standing today, it is operated as a bed and breakfast. About 1869, Joseph Hanmer built Hanmer's Hotel on River Road (Riverside Drive). It burned down in 1873.

Traveling to North Elba by stage was a harrowing enterprise for the early summer tourists. The first and only line until the 1870s began at Westport on Lake Champlain and came through Elizabethtown and Keene following the old Northwest Bay Road, which had come to be known as the Old Military Road. In 1858 the journey from Keene was somewhat facilitated by the construction of a cut-off road through the Cascade Lakes Pass.

North Elba House or Lyon's Inn, opened in 1864 on Old Military Road and still in existence.

The Elizabethtown-North Elba stagecoach.

The original sawmill on Mill Pond, built around 1853.   *(1885 photo)*

Lake Placid House, or Brewster's, 1873, first hotel in Lake Placid Village.

The Golden Age of Hotels

Spurred on by the success of his brother-in-law Joseph Nash, Benjamin Brewster in 1871 built what could be called the first real hotel in what is now the village of Lake Placid. Located at the head of Mirror Lake on the Brewster farmland, it was originally a rather primitive affair known as Lake Placid House, but later grew in size and luxury as the Lake Placid Inn.

The Excelsior House, built 1876, second hotel in Lake Placid Village.

In 1876, Joe Nash followed suit by raising another hotel, the Excelsior House, on the ridge above his Red House. Sold in 1878 to John Stevens and renamed the Stevens House, it burned to the ground on Christmas Eve, 1885. A new Stevens House was immediately built and opened in July of 1886. It would eventually become one of the most famous hotels in the Adirondacks, hosting three United States Presidents and scores of other notables.

Joe Nash saw clearly now what his holdings were meant to hold. He began to sell off his farm. In quick succession, the Grand View, Allen House, Mirror Lake House and Lakeside Inn rose on Nash's hill overlooking Mirror Lake. Main Street made an appearance along Joe's old cow path and shortly after 1880 the first store was built by Frank Stickney across from the present Palace Theater. It housed the first Lake Placid Post Office, with Stickney as post master, in 1883.

Out in the township other hotels were built— Henry VanHoevenberg's great log Adirondack Lodge at Heart Lake and Duncan Cameron's Ray Brook House in Ray Brook. Robert Scott's old wayside inn was enlarged and became the Mountain View House.

Eyes had already turned northward to the beautiful and secluded Placid Lake with its un-inhabited shores and islands. Monroe Hall, prominent Plattsburgh lawyer, built the first summer camp on the east lake in 1870. In 1879, William Fox Leggett built a huge log hotel, known as

Castle Rustico, on the west shore. Also on the west lake, Oliver Abel of Elizabethtown in 1882 erected the Westside, which became the first Whiteface Inn. At the head of the lake was Dr. Charles Alton's Undercliff, a collection of cottages. Somewhat later, the Ruisseaumont was erected on the east lake.

A second stage line was then in operation, leading from the railroad station at AuSable Forks and to North Elba by way of the Wilmington Notch Road, built in 1854. But by 1887 the demise of stage travel was in sight.

Railroad service arrived in Saranac Lake in 1887, and from there tourists bound for North Elba had only a short carriage ride. When the rail line was extended to Lake Placid in 1893, the stagecoach era passed into history.

In 1895, the renowned Lake Placid Club, founded by Dr. Melvin Dewey, New York State Librarian and the inventor of the Dewey Decimal System, opened its doors in a farmhouse known as "Bonnieblink" on the east shore of Mirror Lake. A private institution, the Club was intended as a summer vacation haven for people of modest means from the academic world, but was soon patronized by people of wealth and prominence. Five acres of land and one building soon mushroomed into a vast self-contained complex. Operated year-round, it would serve for many years as the economic base of Lake Placid and enhance its reputation as a first-class resort.

The Lake Placid House "Taxi".

Pioneer farm on Adirondack Lodge Road, 1870s.

View of Main Street, Lake Placid, 1885.
The large building at center is on the site of the present Olympic Arena.

The growth of a settled community had been phenomenal. In 1870 only the Nash and Brewster farms on Mirror Lake and a sawmill on Mill Pond occupied the area around lakes Placid and Mirror. By 1900, the village of Lake Placid was a reality, a nationally recognized summer resort with seven major hotels and many smaller inns and boarding houses, a bustling Main Street, stores and homes, four churches, a public library, golf courses, scores of summer camps on Lake Placid, and railroad service.

A tea party on the Stevens House porch.

PETER MARTIN

Forest View House

Castle Rustico

Lake Placid Inn, enlarged from original Lake Placid House.

The Ruisseaumont

Mirror Lake House

The first Whiteface Inn, originally known as The Westside.

LAKE PLACID-NORTH ELBA HISTORICAL SOCIETY

The Stevens House on August 11, 1897.
Decorated for the visit of President William McKinley.

The Northwoods Inn

The Allen House

Ray Brook House

The Grand View

Adirondack Lodge at Heart Lake

Mountain View House

Lakeside Inn

The American House

The Homestead, Stevens House in background.

Building had commenced at the lower section of the village in the 1880s. A second full-time post office was established there in 1891 in George White's general store, with White as postmaster. It was called "Newman" post office in honor of citizen Annie Newman, which led to a baffling situation.

For the next 45 years, lower Lake Placid village, beginning at the top of Mill Hill, was called Newman, as though it was a separate community. The name began to die out in 1936, when Newman post office closed down. It is known only to old-timers today.

George White's general store, c. 1900. The building still stands at the foot of Mill Hill and is known as "The Handlebar".

Leslie Bennet farm in Cascadeville, late 19th *century.*

Lake Placid Village, c. 1890.
The old Benjamin Brewster farmhouse, known as "the long house" is in the foreground.

View of Lake Placid Village from Mount Whitney, 1897. In the foreground is the Ruisseaumont Hotel.

*Students of the Lake Placid Union School
opposite the Town Hall, 1899.*

Camp Irondequoit on east shore of Lake Placid.

Mill Pond, lower Lake Placid Village, c. 1900.

The name of Lake Placid had been applied to the community at least since 1883, when a United States post office was established in Stickney's store.

It was a consensus of opinion in 1900 that an incorporated village could best meet the needs for management and municipal services.

Local citizens convened at Slater's Hall and formally approved incorporation. Slater's Hall, then serving as the North Elba Town Hall, was housed in a building still standing at the foot of Mill Hill and presently occupied by the Downhill Grill.

On October 20, 1900 with the filing of the necessary documents in the Secretary of State's office, Lake Placid became an incorporated village. Population was then less than 2,000.

An election of officers was held on November 10 and John Shea became Lake Placid's first Mayor, or president, as the office was then called. Shea was an uncle of Olympic speed skater Jack Shea.

Albert H. Billings and Frank Durgan were elected trustees, Howard L. Weaver, treasurer, and Arad B. Stevens, tax collector.

The Board held its first meeting at Slater's Hall on November 17 and appointed Edward Brewster as road commissioner, William Younger as police officer and Charles Forbes as village clerk. The only other business transacted was the passage of a resolution to borrow $500.

The telephone came to Lake Placid in 1901. The village acquired the town of North Elba's sewer system in 1902 and in 1903 purchased from Henry Allen and John and George Stevens their separate waterworks and pipe lines. The present reservoir was soon in place on Mount Whitney.

Lastly, at a cost of $55,000, the village erected a concrete dam on Power Pond, and, just below, its own electric plant with the latest and finest equipment. At 5:20 p.m. on November 18, 1906, Mayor Byron R. Brewster turned a massive wheel at the new powerhouse and the lights came on in Lake Placid.

The town of North Elba now contained a famous resort, but its century-old agrarian culture was by no means at an end. Out in the township, many of the old pioneer farms continued until World War II and beyond, some in the ownership of Lake Placid Club. Potatoes are still grown quite extensively in the fertile North Elba soil.

During this period of enormous growth, another new industry was taking shape in Saranac Lake. Until the late 19th century Saranac Lake had been a jumping-off place for sportsmen venturing into the wilderness, with the Moody boys of North Elba as their most famous guides.

With the arrival of Dr. Edward L. Trudeau in 1875, Saranac Lake's long history as a leading health resort for the treatment of tuberculosis began. North Elba had a role in that industry. Around the turn of the century affluent cure patients began to build sumptuous homes on Saranac Lake's Helen Hill. Cure cottages were also located in North Elba. In 1904, a huge New York State Hospital for the treatment of TB was opened in Ray Brook, leading to the development of the hamlet of Ray Brook.

Lake Placid Club's Forest clubhouses on Mirror Lake.

The steamer "Doris" on Lake Placid, 1900.

Lake Placid Yacht Club. In the background are summer homes
Windy Knowe and High Knoll on Signal Hill.

Lake Placid railroad station, c. 1905.
The hotel carriages are awaiting the arrival of the train.

Original wooden high school, 1900-1922.

On the Wilmington Notch road, 1903.

A Winter Resort Is Born

Ice harness racing on Mirror Lake.

Lake Placid's first winter sport was ice harness racing, dating back to the 1880s. At the turn of the century ice skating was a popular local sport and a boys' hockey team was organized.

In 1896, mainly for the entertainment of TB patients, Saranac Lake began experimenting in ice and snow events, almost unknown in America. The Pontiac Club was organized and a clubhouse was built bordering on Pontiac Bay of Lake Flower in the town of North Elba. Fronting the clubhouse was a skating and hockey rink. In 1897 the club inaugurated the Saranac Lake Winter Carnival, still celebrated today, with a parade, speed and figure skating competitions and snowshoe races. The carnival's ice palace has usually been located in North Elba. Curling was introduced in 1910 and in 1918 an outdoor curling rink appeared on Lake Flower.

But it was in Lake Placid that winter sports took hold in a big way, and it was Melvil Dewey who changed the image of Lake Placid for all time. Melvil Dewey kept his Lake Placid Club open the winter of 1904-1905 for an unprecedented outdoor frolic and ordered 40 pairs of skis from Norway.

St. Eustace Episcopal Church hockey team, 1901.

Pioneers of the first winter outing, Lake Placid Club, 1904-1905.

Mirror Lake rink at Lake Placid.

Ten adventurous Club members came. They skied, skated, tobogganed and snowshoed, the women's petticoats sweeping the drifts, and discovered there were indeed ways to have fun in the snow. So resounding was the success of Dewey's experiment that the Club never again closed its doors on cold weather. A winter sports resort had arrived on the continent.

The growth of winter sports in Lake Placid was as phenomenal as the growth of the village itself. Within 15 years, all manner of facilities were in place at the Club—skating, curling, hockey and ice tennis rinks, ski trails, a double-track toboggan chute and several small ski jumps. By 1921, the Club had a championship caliber ski jump at the site of the present Olympic jumps and was holding national and international contests in addition to cross-country ski races.

Speed skating races were being held in the major cities of the U.S. and Canada at the turn of the century, but it was not long before Saranac Lake and Lake Placid began to dominate the sport. Major races were held on the Pontiac rink as early as 1912, and beginning in 1918 the great Mirror Lake rink was the locale of such events as the Eastern, North American and Diamond Trophy races.

It was speed skating that brought Lake Placid its first great national publicity. The local Speed Skating Association developed a remarkable stable of young skaters who won everything in sight. Out of this group came native sons Charles Jewtraw

and Jack Shea, gold medal winners in the 1924 and 1932 Olympics respectively.

Lake Placid's Charles Jewtraw, gold medal winner at first Winter Olympics in Chamonix, France, 1924.

Taking the bumps on the Lake Placid Club golf course.

The glamour and excitement of those speed skating days have never been duplicated in Lake Placid, not even by two Olympic Winter Games. But after the Lake Placid Ski Club was organized in 1921, skiing became the dominant sport.

Speed skating races on Mirror Lake, 1919.
Note large number of spectators, including those on rooftops.

Pontiac rink in Saranac Lake.

Lake Placid Village and the lakes in winter as seen from Grand View Hill, c. 1903.

Looking down at upper Main Street, 1903.

View of Main Street, Lake Placid, in 1903. First building in background is the Lake Placid Public Library. Note plank sidewalk.

Main Street, Lake Placid, in 1906.

Ski class, early 1920s.
Instructor at left is the famous "Jackrabbit" Johannsen.

Ice gymkhana, Lake Placid Club, c. 1917.

Skating on Mirror Lake opposite present bandshell park, c. 1918.

Lake Placid itself continued to grow, along with the winter sports phenomenon. Many new buildings appeared on Main Street, including the Palace Theater and the Marcy Hotel. The "great Main Street fire" of January 1919 destroyed four business blocks which were soon replaced. In 1922, students moved into a new brick school, now the south wing of the Lake Placid Central School. The original Town Hall, built in 1905, succumbed to fire in 1915 and was replaced immediately by the present brick structure.

Brick high school erected in 1922, now the south wing of the Lake Placid Central School.

LAKE PLACID-NORTH ELBA HISTORICAL SOCIETY

The village toboggan slide on Signal Hill, c. 1910.

One of the small ski jumps on the Lake Placid Club golf course, 1915.

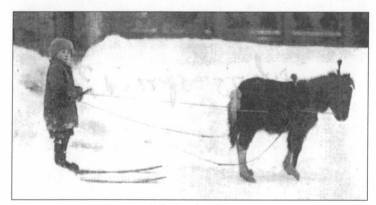

Who's afraid ?

A good many homes were also built, both within and on the outskirts of Lake Placid. Luxurious camps continued to rise on the shores of Placid Lake and commodious summer homes were erected on Signal and Grand View hills. Among the best-loved of Placid's summer residents was Victor Herbert, the noted composer of operettas, who occupied his Camp Joyland on Lake Placid from 1905 until his death in 1925.

Summer homes began to appear on Signal Hill, c. 1903. Lake Placid Inn is at right.

Victor Herbert, beloved summer resident.
LAKE PLACID-NORTH ELBA HISTORICAL SOCIETY

Upper Main Street, Lake Placid, c. 1920.

Main Street, Lake Placid, after the big snowstorm of January 30, 1925.

GROVER CLEVELAND, PHOTOGRAPHER

Upper Lake Placid Village, c. 1920. From left to right on top of hill—St. Agnes Catholic Church, Stevens House Annex, Stevens House. At middle right is Lakeside Inn.

Over at the Lake Placid Club in 1928, Godfrey Dewey, son of Melvil, was convinced that Lake Placid now possessed the expertise and organization necessary to host a Winter Olympics. He sold the village and town fathers on the idea. On March 29, 1929, as Lake Placid's sole delegate, he sailed for France to bid for the III Olympic Winter Games of 1932 against such sites as California's Yosemite, Canada and Norway. Astonishingly, Dewey came home with the big prize.

In spite of the major depression that soon engulfed the country, the next three years saw great activity here. A bobsled run, indoor ice arena and outdoor skating oval were constructed. The ski jump was overhauled, and a network of new cross-country trails was designed. Alpine skiing was not yet on the Olympic agenda.

Opening ceremonies, III Olympic Winter Games, 1932.

The III Olympic Winter Games were held February 4 through the 13th, 1932. Governor Franklin D. Roosevelt presided over the simple opening ceremonies. The Olympic torch pageantry was as yet unknown and the raising of the Olympic flag signaled that the Games had begun. They were a success. In the grip of the great world depression and plagued by a lack of snow, this little village had persevered and carried the day. As an added bonus, its own Curtis and J. Hubert Stevens won a gold medal in the two-man bobsledding and its own Jack Shea won two gold medals in speed skating, proving to the world that Lake Placid was the home of champions.

Governor Franklin D. Roosevelt at the opening of the 1932 Winter Olympics.

Olympic ski jump and spectators
1932 Winter Olympics.

*Lake Placid's J. Hubert Stevens, driver, and Curtis Stevens,
winners of gold medal in 2-man bobsledding
1932 Winter Olympics.*

*Lake Placid's Jack Shea,
winner of two gold medals at the
1932 Winter Olympics.*

Between Olympics
1932-1980

The Olympic Arena advertises summer ice season.

The half century following the 1932 Olympics was a time of slow change, a confirmation of Lake Placid's status as a top summer and winter resort, and a widening of its horizons. In the continuing years of the Great Depression, the Olympic Arena proved an economic boon. Large conventions were soon booked. Immediately, in the summer of 1932, the rink was opened for the first summer ice season, which has continued uninterrupted into the year 2000. For close to 70 years, figure skating hopefuls from all parts of the country have spent the summer training at Lake Placid, and instructors such as the great Gus Lussi and Howard Nicholson have produced national, world and Olympic notables.

Since 1932, the Olympic Arena has also been the setting for one of Lake Placid's great traditions—the annual crowning of the King and Queen of Winter.

In those early years the most elaborate summer figure skating shows offered anywhere were staged at the arena and drew national attention. The ice was painted in vivid colors and glamorous sets, designed by the talented arena manager, H. L. (Jack) Garren, were constructed for each skating

Summer ice operetta in the Olympic Arena, August, 1935.

operetta. These extravaganzas continued until the late 1940s.

A large addition to the arena, with a second rink, opened in 1967.

With the only bobsled run on the continent, the town became the national capital of bobsledding.

Local and area men soon mastered the sport and dominated the U.S. Olympic and World teams for 24 years, until 1956. Ivan E. Brown and Alan M. Washbond of neighboring Keene Valley won the gold medals in two-man bobsledding in 1936 in Garmisch-Partenkirchen, Germany. Francis Tyler's four-man bobsled team of Lake Placid won America's last gold medal in the sport at the 1948 Winter Olympics in St. Moritz, Switzerland.

The 1932 Olympics had touched off a great explosion in downhill skiing in the United States. Major ski centers were cropping up everywhere, but, strangely, Lake Placid was lagging far behind. It had a unique handicap. It was hemmed in by the high peaks of the State's Forest Preserve. This is "forever wild" land, protected by the State Constitution. Not a tree could be cut without approval of two legislatures and the approval of the electorate.

In the ski train era of the 1930s, Lake Placid had to make do with a few small ski centers, such as Scott's Cobble and Fawn Ridge, located within the town limits.

At last, in 1941, after much effort on the part of Lake Placid promoters, the voters of New York State approved the construction of a major ski center on Whiteface Mountain.

World War II intervened and it was not until 1949 that the center opened on Marble Mountain, a shoulder of Whiteface, and Lake Placid became a contender in the alpine skiing craze. It was soon learned that Marble Mountain was plagued by unfavorable wind conditions and a new site had to be found.

With a helping hand from Governor Averill Harriman, a second constitutional amendment was approved, and in January of 1958, today's magnificent Whiteface Mountain Ski Center opened.

While geographically in the town of Wilmington, and nine miles distant, Whiteface is a distinct feature of Lake Placid's winter program.

In this era, local children received a special training in all winter sports. Many noteworthy young athletes came out of these programs to star in State and national competitions.

Lake Placid's famous junior ski jumpers and their trainers—
Left, John Viscome and right, Bud Colby.

Taking the curve on the Olympic bobrun.

Scott's Cobble ski center.

Elegant horse shows were an important part of Lake Placid life in the '30s and '40s but continued only until World War II. In 1970, Mrs. Ruth Newberry of AuSable Forks staged a children's Pony Club show at Lake Placid and the next year, 1971, a full-fledged equestrian event, which has continued to the present day. Permanent horse show grounds have been the setting for the annual Lake Placid and I Love New York horse shows, held back to back. Now televised nationally, they are premier and prestigious events on the Grand Prix circuit and attract the best riders from all over North America.

©Photo courtesy of Classic Communications

Lake Placid Horse Show grounds.
CLASSIC COMMUNICATIONS

While the '32 Olympics did not foster a huge building boom, the landscape was slowly changing. The old wooden hotels and inns of the golden age began to vanish and were replaced by that new breed of accommodations, motels, large and small, modest and grand. Vacation patterns and vacationers themselves took on a new look. Few visitors now came for an entire summer, and once exclusively a resort of the wealthy and famous, Lake Placid now attracted all manner of guests as general prosperity evolved.

The town and village also reached out in new directions, outside the perimeter of sports.

In the '50s and '60s, the TB industry, for over 50 years the mainstay of Saranac Lake and Ray Brook, collapsed. With the discovery of highly effective drug treatment, bed rest and the balsam-scented Adirondack air were no longer requisites. Ray Brook State Hospital remained open as a drug treatment center for women and later became a correctional institution. In the North Elba section of Saranac Lake, the famed Will Rogers Memorial Hospital (originally the National Variety Artists Lodge) turned from the treatment of TB to the treatment of other lung diseases. It closed in 1974. The building now houses an upscale retirement apartment complex for seniors.

Will Rogers Memorial Hospital in Saranac Lake.

A sizeable health center, Placid Memorial Hospital, opened in Lake Placid in 1951, followed by the Uihlein Mercy Center, a state-of-the-art nursing home and rehabilitation facility for the aged, in 1968. Both were made possible through generous donations from the entire community.

The sole educational facilities, aside from public schools, had been Northwood School, still in existence, a prep school for boys, founded in 1905, and Montemare School for girls, of short duration. Now the area seriously entered the field of education with the prestigious and private North Country School for elementary boarding students, located in Cascadeville, the North Country Community College at Saranac Lake, St. Agnes Parochial School, and, in the 1970s, the Mountain House School at Lake Placid, a private prep school for student athletes, now known as the National Sports Academy.

Through the generosity of Henry Uihlein, Cornell University established an experimental potato farm and then an experimental maple syrup plantation, on Bear Cub Road. Through the generosity of Mrs. W. Alton Jones (Mrs. Nettie Marie Jones), the W. Alton Jones Cell Science Center for tissue culture was built, as well as the handsome Lake Placid Center for the Arts, now a significant seat of culture for music, dance, motion pictures, theater, and art exhibits, and featuring Lake Placid's distinguished little symphony orchestra, the Sinfonietta.

The community's dream of holding another Winter Olympics would not die. Avid groups prepared bids for all the Winter Olympics from 1956 through 1976, but were bypassed. Meanwhile, Lake Placid hosted many outstanding competitions, such as world and national championships in a variety of sports, and the Kennedy Memorial International Winter Games. Most importantly, it was awarded the World University Games, the biggest winter sports competition in the world other than the Olympics.

The World University Games held at Lake Placid in 1972 was a huge, rollicking, noisy and fun-filled spectacle and in some ways more enjoyable and profitable than the '32 Olympics. And, this time there was a wealth of snow.

The 1980 Olympics would soon be up for bid, and this time Lake Placid was determined to make a presentation that could not be ignored. In October of 1974, a delegation of 16, along with crates of material and a cheering section of perhaps 60 people, proceeded to Vienna to bid for the 1980 Games. It was in sharp contrast to Lake Placid's bid for the '32 Games—one delegate, Godfrey Dewey, who carried a few notes and sketches in his pockets.

Again the little village in the Adirondacks won the prize. The 1980 Olympic Winter Games were awarded to Lake Placid.

A World-Class Resort

90 and 120-meter Olympic ski jumps, XIII Olympic Winter Games at Lake Placid, 1980.

NANCIE BATTAGLIA

Huge preparations began and continued over the next five years. A large field house for hockey and figure skating, a new refrigerated speed skating oval, repairs to the arena and renovation of the town hall transformed the center of Lake Placid village.

Out at Mt. VanHoevenberg, the bobsled run was reconditioned and refrigerated, a refrigerated luge track was built, and extensive trails were constructed for the cross-country skiing and biathlon events. The old ski jump was replaced by two new 90 and 120-meter jumps towering over the landscape. Whiteface Mountain Ski Center was greatly improved and an athlete's village was built at Ray Brook.

It was a far cry, both in time and essence, from the homey III Olympic Winter Games of 1932 to the XIII Olympic Winter Games of 1980 with their pageantry, hordes of events, athletes and spectators, and the publicity mass-produced by television and some 3500 members of the press.

The two events, separated by 48 years, had one common denominator—a lack of snow. It was of little consequence in 1980 with all the new snow-making devices.

A transportation blunder marred the 1980 Games. It is long forgotten. The words "Lake Placid 1980" evoke only that stunning "miracle on ice", when the underdog U.S. hockey squad, a collection of brash young collegians, who learned to skate on frozen ponds, defeated the awesome Soviet Union team. Americans needed some cheering up and the victory set off a wild celebration throughout the country. It perhaps will always be regarded as one of the greatest upsets of the modern Olympics. The U.S. went on to win the gold medal in hockey and five gold medals for Eric Heiden's speed skating.

"Miracle on Ice"
The United States hockey team celebrates its victory.
1980 Winter Olympics.   Lake Placid North Elba Historical Society

One important legacy of 1980 has been Lake Placid's designation as the Eastern Olympic Training Center. A fine housing and training facility for Olympic hopefuls is situated on Old Military Road.

Great change and development have come to Lake Placid and North Elba within the last twenty years. This remarkable renaissance is almost entirely due to the worldwide exposure and publicity afforded by the 1980 Olympic Winter Games.

The area seems not so much to have been revitalized as to have been reinvented. While the backdrop of ancient mountains is eternal, Lake Placid and North Elba have taken on a new personality, engaging and exciting, without sacrificing their small-town ambience.

An enormous building boom, that still continues, has brought a variety of new accommodations and houses, well-regulated by the village, town and Adirondack Park Agency.

Whiteface Mountain Ski Center,
1980 Winter Olympics.

NANCIE BATTAGLIA

The last of the golden age hotels have vanished from the landscape—Whiteface Inn and the sprawling Lake Placid Club.

Replacing those grand old hotels of yesteryear are the larger inns and motor inns of today, some of which stand on the old sites. These include the Holiday Inn-Lake Placid Resort at the former Grand View Hotel site and the Lake Placid Hilton on the old Homestead grounds.

Today's Mirror Lake Inn lies between the former Lakeside Inn and Brewster's original Lake Placid House. Condominiums occupy the site of old Whiteface Inn. St. Moritz Hotel is a 1926 enlargement of a small inn, The Pines, which opened in 1900.

The last of the open lands, especially the Averyville section, are being rapidly colonized, not only by local residents but by retirees and second home owners. The retirement and second home invasion has been largely responsible for the demise of the historic two-season character of the region. Activity now abounds in all seasons of the year.

Probably the most telling change is that of Lake Placid's main business section, upper Main Street. Once primarily the habitat of local service stores, groceries, pharmacies, garages and gas stations, it is now given over entirely to the visitor—a tourist's paradise of boutiques and specialty shops featuring unique merchandise and clothing, as well as food bars and restaurants.

State government now significantly impacts the economy.

The hamlet of Ray Brook seems almost an extension of the State Campus at Albany, with substantial buildings housing the Adirondack Park Agency, State Police Troop B headquarters, and Region 5 headquarters of the Department of Environmental Conservation. There is also the Meadowbrook State Campsite, and the old Ray Brook Hospital is now a State correctional facility. As well, the former Olympic athlete village serves as a Federal correctional facility.

In the Lake Placid area, the State's Olympic Regional Development Authority, with additional funding from the town of North Elba, finances and operates the Olympic venues for athlete training and competition and for public enjoyment.

Major competitions of national and world status continue, including the recently introduced Empire State Winter Games, and the area has reached out in a bewildering number of new directions, both cultural and sports oriented.

In 2000 alone, Lake Placid was chosen to host the Isuzu Ironman Triathlon, the very first Winter Goodwill Games and ESPN's delightful summer presentation, the Great Outdoor Games. Sponsors of international events have suddenly recognized the town's singular assets for television coverage— the impressive scenic setting and sports venues, apart from its well-known prowess in organization and production.

Lake Placid is now the national headquarters of

the U.S. Bobsled and Skeleton Federation, the U.S. Luge Association, as well as the North American headquarters of the Ironman.

A new organization, Lake Placid Institute for the Arts and Humanities, has brought fresh and stimulating cultural activity, featuring Music, Ethnic and "Writers in Residence" seminars, photography workshops and a children's poetry contest, attracting a new breed of participants from all over America.

Lake Placid's first Film Festival in the summer of 2000 was so well attended that it may become a permanent fixture.

The summer of 2000 was also highlighted by the vacation visit of President and Mrs. William Clinton and daughter, Chelsea, and the announcement that

President William Jefferson Clinton and admirers.
Lake Placid, August 2000.

the U.S. National women's hockey team was moving to Lake Placid for an 18-month training period.

A new Lake Placid 1932 and 1980 Winter Olympic Museum, situated in the 1980 Olympic Center, has joined the Lake Placid-North Elba Historical Society's picturesque little museum, located in the former local railroad station, in dispensing the history of Lake Placid and North Elba.

On the threshold of this new Millennium, Lake Placid is a name recognized around the world, and the world is beating a path to Lake Placid.

Success has its reasons. The area has been blessed with two singular assets beyond its natural physical endowments. The first has been the ability of its people to recognize change as opportunity and to seize upon it. The second, and most valuable, has been the volunteer effort and wholehearted involvement of its people in all civic endeavors and events. This very strong volunteer spirit has been around for a long time and is passed, like the Olympic torch, from generation to generation.

It has been a long and eventful journey from the little wilderness outpost known as The Plains of Abraham to the world-class village of Lake Placid and town of North Elba.

The new field house, far left, and the skating oval dominate central Lake Placid village.
1980 Winter Olympics.

MAYORS OF THE VILLAGE OF LAKE PLACID

John Shea	1900-1904
Byron R. Brewster	1904-1908
John A. Stevens	1908-1910
Frank G. Walton	1910-1914
James B. Hurley	1914-1916
Fred Dashnaw	1916-1917
Frank Leonard	1917-1918
Patrick J. Hennessy	1919-1922
Frederick Isham	1922-1924
Frank Leonard	1924-1925
Frank Fay	1925-1927
William Feek	1927-1929
Martin Ryan	1929-1933
George C. Owens	1933-1941
Luke L. Perkins	1941-1949
Ernest G. Dodds	1949-1952
Harlan K. Hunkins	1952-1953
George C. Owens	1953-10/24/57
Ernest H. Holt	11/4/57-3/18/58
William J. Hurley	1958-1959
Robert J. Peacock	1959-1993
Shirley W. Seney	1993-1995
T. James Strack	1996-2001
Robert Politi	2001-

SUPERVISORS OF THE TOWN OF NORTH ELBA

1850	John Thompson
1851-1852	Timothy Nash
1853-1855	Daniel Ames
1856	Daniel Osgood
1857	Milo Merrill
1858-1859	Daniel Ames
1860-1862	Milote Baker
1863	Daniel Ames
1864-1865	Timothy S. Nash
1866-1867	Daniel Ames
1868	Alexis Hinckley
1869-1870	Andrew J. Baker
1871-1872	Joseph V. Nash
1873-1874	Moses S. Ames
1875-1876	Judson C. Ware
1877	Myron T. Brewster
1878-1879	Moses S. Ames
1880-1881	Byron R. Brewster
1882	Benjamin T. Brewster
1883-1884	Henry Allen
1885-1886	George A. Stevens
1887-1890	George T. Chellis
1891-1892	Robert Ames
1893-1895	George E. White
1896-1897	Edward L. Ware
1898	Walter S. Wood
1899-1900	George T. Chellis
1901-1902	Walter S. Wood
1903-1906	James Shea
1907-1911	Benjamin W. Lewis
1912-1917	John F. White
1918-1947	Willis Wells
1948-1959	Harold Soden
1960-1973	William Hurley
1974-1981	Jack Shea
1982-1995	Matthew Clark
1996-	Shirley Seney

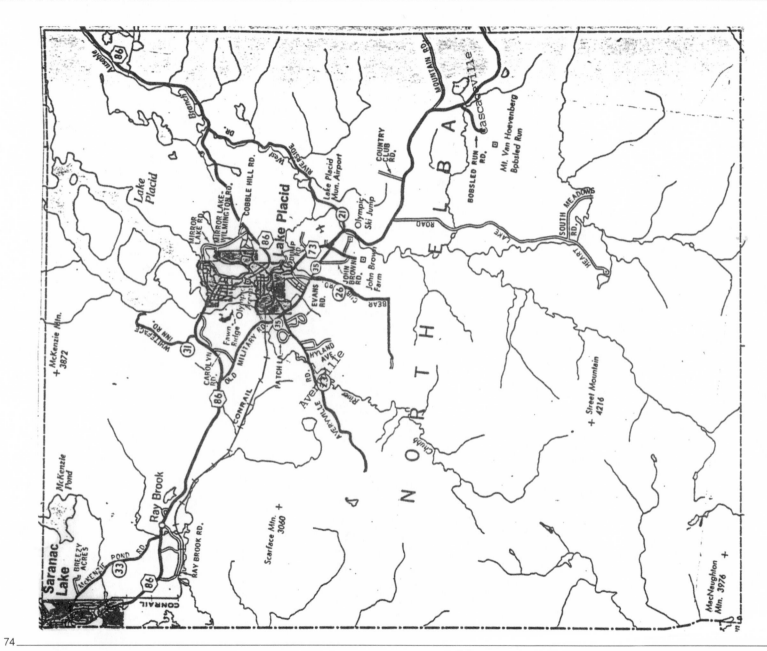